WE WIN NOW LET'S BATTLE

Be Equipped with God's tools for battle

Dawn Cordova & Roxanne Dexter

WestBow Press books may be ordered through booksellers or by contacting:

WestBow Press
A Division of Thomas Nelson & Zondervan
1663 Liberty Drive
Bloomington, IN 47403
www.westbowpress.com
844-714-3454

Scripture quotations are taken from the Holy Bible, New Living Translation, copyright ©1996, 2004, 2015 by Tyndale House Foundation. Used by permission of Tyndale House Publishers, Carol Stream, Illinois 60188. All rights reserved.

ISBN: 978-1-6642-4550-1 (sc)
ISBN: 978-1-6642-4551-8 (e)

Library of Congress Control Number: 2021919478

Print information available on the last page.

WestBow Press rev. date: 12/06/2021

WESTBOW
PRESS®
A DIVISION OF THOMAS NELSON
& ZONDERVAN

Contents

Wave Your Banner of Faith and Commitment to the Lord
    Praise the Lord
    Sweet Surrender
    Obedience
    Prayer

Bow in Humble Adoration
    Be Humble
    Forgiveness
    Love One Another

Be The Salt And Light in This World
    Sacrifice Is Worship
    Serve Others
    Overflowing Joy
    Freedom
    Rest in Him

Preface

When the Lord placed this on our hearts to write this study, He had only said the word, "Book," to me a few weeks earlier, and I quickly pushed it away. I was in the beginning of one of the darkest times of my life, when God had stripped me of all the idols and titles that I had placed before Him. I was at work that Friday when Dawn called me, and in her always joyful, bubbly voice said, "Hey, Rox, do you wanna do something with me?" and of course, my natural response was, "What?" though I was hesitant because of the place I was in. Dawn continued, "I've been looking for and praying about a Bible study. The Lord spoke to my heart and said, 'Write it.' I want you to pray about it and see if you want to write it with me."

Well, three and a half years later, this study is now finished. It has been a battle, but this battle I would not change for the world. I have learned to use the very tools that God gave me, fighting the good fight and placing His truth in my heart, knowing I will reap a harvest of blessings as I hang in there, trusting in the Lord. Walking this study out in my life while writing it, God is sanctifying me from the inside out, and I am becoming real with the Lord. My relationship with Jesus is more intimate and personal than ever before. I'm saying no to me and yes to God. In all of it, I give God the glory!

For me, I can honestly say the battle is real. The more we use the tools that God has given us to pursue this life on earth, the wiser we become to the tricks of the enemy. As I reflect,

I remember when God lifted me up from the pit of despair, out of my miry clay, set my feet on a solid rock, and made my steps firm. It was not easy. As matter of fact, it was a hard time in my life. But the moment I cried out to God that I needed Him and couldn't do life without Him was the beginning of a long journey of pursuing Jesus instead of pursuing the world. As I took the steps to find out who God was in my life, He showed up every single time. I felt an overwhelming sense of love and presence from my Father in heaven that kept me in pursuit of all that He has for me. As my granddaughter always says, "Hold you, Gramma," Jesus is there to hold you as you journey through life with Him. Today all I can say is not to give up. Pursue Jesus with all that you are, and He will be exalted in your life.

We felt every word that was written, though hard at times. We prayed, we listened, then we acted. Our hearts were to allow God to write this study in order to equip you with the tools to overcome the enemy and live an abundant life. We pray God's gracious hand upon you: Hang on! Hang in! Hold on tightly, and believe as you battle with these tools given to you in the study! Keep your eyes on Jesus; always look through the lenses of God's goodness and God's faithfulness! Our prayer for you is that you keep on keeping on until the day Jesus calls you home, always in love and always being humble. He's got you, mighty warriors!

We dedicate this study to our Lord and Savior Jesus! Honor and glory to You forever!

ALLOW

GOD TO

CHANGE

YOUR

HEART

IN A

SEASON

Do You Believe?

You Are a Soul on the Search

There is going to be a time in your life, if it has not happened already, when you will ask yourself, "What is this life about? Why are we here?" You will feel a nudging that leads you to ponder about this world we live in. It doesn't matter what walk of life you're living, God is trying to get your attention. Every single one of us longs to feel whole. It's as if our souls are searching to find fullness, meaning, contentment, and purpose for our lives. Most often we turn toward the things of this world, trying anything that will boost our egos or make us feel numb, only to end up feeling empty all over again. Until we are united with our Creator, we will always search for the one thing that makes us feel whole, for the one thing that will overwhelm and satisfy our souls. This one thing remains: It's God's love for us and His only Son, Jesus, who saves.

> *"If you confess with your mouth that Jesus is Lord and believe in your heart that God raised him from the dead, you will be saved. For it is by believing in your heart that you are made right with God, and it is by confessing with your mouth that you are saved."* (Romans 10:9–10)

Jesus made a way for you and me to commune with our heavenly Father. When we make the choice to ask Jesus into our hearts, our spirits become God's spirit, and our souls are reunited with the One who created us. We are one with the Lord! God has made His way into our hearts, creating fullness for our souls where there once was a void. Get ready, for your cup will overflow with God's goodness and supply you with everything you need and much more.

"And this same God who takes care of me will supply all your needs from his glorious riches, which have been given to us in Christ Jesus." (Philippians 4:19)

Ask yourself, "Do I believe?"

Do I believe that God created me from the dust of this earth?

Do I believe in the heavenly Father, who loves me so much that He sent His Son to die on a cross for my sins?

Do I believe in the everlasting Father, who wants to walk this life with me?

Do I believe that God is actually preparing a place for me right now in paradise for all eternity?

Ask yourself, "Do I believe?" Believing is an action you take to express your commitment to Jesus. It is being bold as you come to Him, humbly knowing you need God in your life.

Listen to what Jesus tells us in John 11:25–26: *"I am the resurrection and the life. Anyone who believes in me will live, even after dying. Everyone who lives in me and believes in me will never ever die."*

Do you believe this, _____? As you write your name in the blank, take this time to pray and ask our Lord and Savior Jesus to reveal Himself to you. As your sisters in Christ, know that we are praying this very moment for you as you take this time to seek Him.

Scriptures to study: Genesis 1, 2, 3; John 3:16; Acts 16:31.

Journal

Faith

"So faith comes from hearing, that is, hearing the Good News about Christ."

Romans 10:17

God gives each of us a measure of faith. This measure is a gift from God. By hearing the Word of God, our faith will grow. *"And it is impossible to please God without faith. Anyone who wants to come to him must believe that God exists and that he rewards those who sincerely seek him."* (Hebrews 11:6) A faith that steadily progresses from this measure into a great, strong faith is pleasing to God. I believe because I heard and was given a measure of faith. Faith is the ground of our salvation and given to us out of His abundance of grace. Faith involves confident action in response to what God has made known. Take your measure and grow with it!

"Faith is the confidence that what we hope for will actually happen; it gives us assurance about things we cannot see." (Hebrews 11:1) Faith completely knows that God is who He says He is and that He will do what He says He will do in our lives. In every situation, have faith and know that God exists and is working His will in your life. Philemon 1:6 says, *"And I am praying that you will put into action the generosity that comes from your faith as you understand and experience all the good things we have in Christ."*

So let the fellowship of your faith become effective through your knowledge of every good thing that is in you for Christ Jesus. Listen to the very heart of God for you in Jeremiah 29:11, *"'For I know the plans I have for you,' says the Lord. 'They are plans for good and not for disaster, to give you a future and a hope.'"* Wow! Hope is a confident expectation of what God has promised.

God is an anchor for your soul! Stand firm in the faith! Be courageous! Be strong, and hold onto God's promises! Spend time each and every day in His Word, seeking out who He is. Believe and have faith knowing that He is walking your life with you. Know at this very moment that God *is* revealing Himself to you. Know at this very moment that God *is* showing you who He is.

Scriptures to study: 1 Corinthians 16:13; Ephesians 4:11–16; John 20:29.

Journal

Trusting in God

Whom do I depend on, myself or God? Who controls my life, myself or God? Is my life all about me or God? Do I allow God to take over my life and my flesh, or do I hold on to my life and my flesh and do things my way? Trust is hard to do without the help of the Lord. Life tends to throw many disappointments and broken promises at us without warning. While desiring a life full of goodness, we find ourselves building up walls to protect ourselves. It seems as though the more we long for love, the more we encounter the things of the world. Before we know it, we are living in the world bound by its darkness. Hopelessness takes root, and since we feel defeated, unloved, and broken, we put up our defenses. Living behind our walls so we don't get hurt, we guard our hearts, and no one enters. Keep out! There will come a day when your walls will come crashing down. Be encouraged! Love is going to change you!

Psalm 25:1 says, *"Oh Lord, I give my life to you. I trust in you, my God!"* It's a decision we make to trust in the Lord. We choose not to respond in our flesh but to wait on the Lord. Our flesh wants to worry, fret, and control everything in every situation. God wants us to submit our lives to Him and completely depend on Him. The more we trust the Lord, the more His spirit becomes a part of us. Proverbs 3:5–6 tell us to *"Trust in the Lord with all your heart; do not depend on your own understanding. Seek His will in all you do and he will show you which path to take."* God desires us to depend on Him for everything we do, need, and want. Step back, and don't get in the way of what God wants to do. Allow God to take control over your life, and watch how God will be glorified!

This lifestyle of trusting God gives true inner peace, and it sets our feet on solid ground. *"What shall we say about such wonderful things as these? If God is for us, who can ever be against us*?"(Romans 8:31) Rest assured, friends, that our God is who He says He is, and He has every good intention for you and for your life here on earth. We love you and want to leave you with this:

"Don't worry about anything; instead, pray about everything. Tell God what you need, and thank him for all he has done. Then you will experience God's peace, which exceeds anything we can understand. His peace will guard your hearts and minds as you live in Christ Jesus." (Philippians 4:6–7)

Scriptures to study: Hebrews 10:23; 1 Peter 1:3–9; Isaiah 12:2.

Journal

BE

A

FORTRESS

FOR THE

LORD

Preparing for Battle: Let's Get Dressed

Millions of people put on a uniform every day without giving it a second thought. My son, for instance, is a police officer and puts on a tactical uniform for duty. This uniform includes a bulletproof vest with a camera, protective boots, and a belt that holds handcuffs, a Taser and handheld protective devices, pepper spray, a radio, ammunition, and a flashlight. Why? To protect! My daughter, who is a nurse, also wears a uniform every day. This consists of hospital-issued scrubs, a stethoscope, protective eyewear, gloves, a mask, and coverings for her head and feet. Why? To protect!

As believers, Ephesians 6:14–17 tells us exactly what to wear:

> *"Stand your ground, putting on the belt of truth and the body armor of God's righteousness. For shoes, put on the peace that comes from the Good News so that you will be fully prepared. In addition to all of these, hold up the shield of faith to stop the fiery arrows of the devil. Put on salvation as your helmet, and take the sword of the Spirit, which is the word of God."*

Why? Because we are not fighting against flesh-and-blood enemies but against evil rulers and authorities of the unseen world, against mighty powers in this dark world, and against evil spirits in the heavenly places.

Truth, righteousness, peace, faith, and salvation are all gifts of God to us. They are defensive in nature for our protection. The sword of the Spirit, which is the Word of God, is given to us to be used as an offensive weapon for our protection. All the pieces of the armor belong to and come from Him.

The truth of who God is and the action of His written Word, which is alive and powerful, work in harmony to bring life to anyone who believes. *"A final word; Be strong in the Lord and in his mighty power."* (Ephesians 6:10)

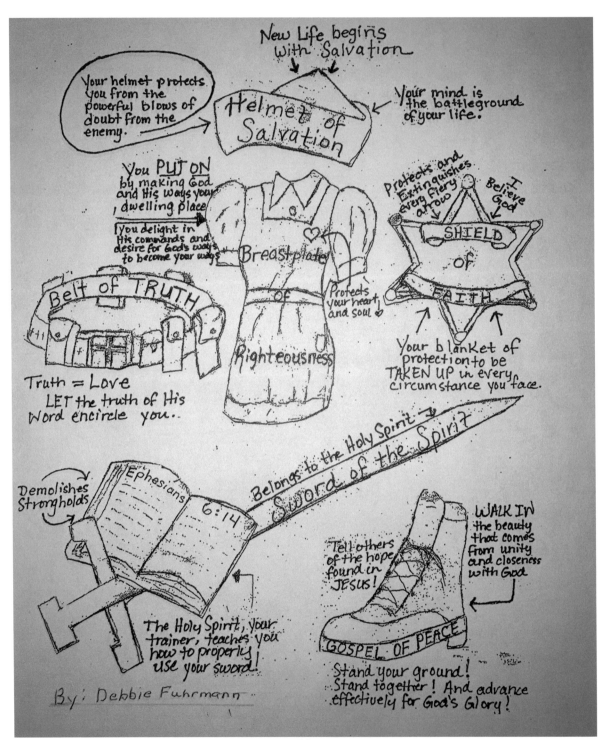

Journal

The Belt of Truth

The belt of truth is the first piece of the full armor of God. Without truth we are lost. Jesus says, *"I am the way, the truth, and the life."* (John 14:6) It is only through Jesus that we come to God. Therefore, truth is of the utmost importance in the life of a believer. Without truth, the rest of the armor is of no use to us because the belt—truth—holds all the armor together under pressure in battle.

It is one's responsibility to "put on" the belt of truth and to cinch the belt tightly around the waist with the truth of God's Word. We must anchor ourselves in Christ and scripture, which provide the protection and ability that we will need to stand our ground. We are to embrace this truth actively and use it. God has given us an advocate, the spirit of truth, which is a crucial piece of defensive armor guarding our innermost beings in the battles against the lies and deceptions of the enemy.

This belt will protect and prepare you for the battles that are part of every believer's life. Believers who walk with Jesus are secure because they know the cross has broken the devil's power, and the Lord protects them! Buckle your belt tightly every day. Pray for complete understanding of God's truth so you will be productive in battle.

Starting today, commit a time to spend reading God's Word.

Scriptures to study: Colossians 3:14–15; 1 John 4:4; 2:14.

Journal

Breastplate of Righteousness

The breastplate of righteousness, which is attached to the belt, applies the truth of the Bible to our lives. The breastplate protects our hearts and vital organs from the attacks of the enemy.

Our hearts are susceptible to the wickedness of this world. Without protection we leave ourselves exposed to the enemy's lies and deception. Satan wants us to compromise the truth by giving into unrighteous living. We are to be unshakable and uncompromising in our moral lives. When Jesus died on the cross, His righteousness was credited to all who believe in Him. We are righteous only through Jesus, who protects His children with the armor of God. Put on your new self.

> *"The night is almost gone; the day of salvation will soon be here. So remove your dark deeds like dirty clothes, and put on the shining armor of right living."* (Romans 13:12)

End today's lesson spending some time with the Lord. Pray that He will reveal and heal your dirty laundry.

Scriptures to study: Proverbs 3:5; Romans 5:18–19; Ephesians 4:24.

Journal

Put on Your Shoes

"Then you will experience God's peace, which exceeds anything we can understand. His peace will guard your hearts and minds as you live in Christ Jesus."

Philippians 4:7

There is such a peace knowing the Word of God, proclaiming His truth, and sharing the gospel. We must be firmly planted in God's truth with faith securing our shoes of peace with every wrap of the laces. As we walk life out with each step, no matter what we face, we are called to walk as Jesus did. We remain peaceful as we boldly share the good news of Jesus, who ultimately protects us in this battle. Staying in constant communion with Him brings the peace that passes all understanding. God is our rock, our solid rock of salvation. Stand confident and joyful in His peace.

"Then Christ will make his home in your hearts as you trust in him. Your roots will grow down into God's love and keep you strong." (Ephesians 3:17)

As you battle this ground, God's peace gives us His ability to enjoy the very life He created for us. Put on your shoes of peace, and be ready to spread the good news of the gospel. Share in the joy of His presence, and glorify our Lord with each step of your life.

Scriptures to study: Philippians 4:4–7; John 14:27; Numbers 6:24–26.

Journal

Shield of Faith

This shield symbolizes the beautiful coming together of our beliefs, our faiths, and our trust in the One who created it all! You see, God is our shield. *"The Lord is my rock, my fortress, and my savior; my God is my rock, in whom I find protection. He is my shield, the power that saves me, and my place of safety."* (Psalm 18:2)

We are told in Ephesians 6:16 to "*hold up the shield of faith to stop the fiery arrows of the devil.*" We know that God defeated the devil and won the war. Hold up your shield of faith believing God is doing everything beyond your shield to protect you from the schemes of the enemy. We find refuge in God alone, and He is our blanket of protection in all circumstances. "*How precious is your unfailing love, O God! All humanity finds shelter in the shadow of your wings.*" (Psalm 36:7)

God loves you so much that it was you He thought of when He gave His one and only Son, Jesus. Stand strong in your faith, set your mind on the things above, hold your shield high, and watch the devil flee in Jesus's name.

Keep your shield up! God is fighting your battle!

Scriptures to study: 2 Corinthians 5:7; 1 John 5:5; Psalm 91.

Journal

Salvation as Your Helmet

"Let all the world look to me for salvation!
For I am God; there is no other."

Isaiah 45:22

Salvation is the saving grace from death and being separated from God. Jesus is our only hope to deliver us from the power and effects of sin. God has given us dominion and authority over our minds through the gift of salvation.

The helmet protects our minds from the onslaught of doubts from the enemy. Place the helmet of salvation on your head, and allow only what is of the Lord to enter. Secure your salvation in Jesus, and let Him be sovereign over your well-being, believing Jesus made the ultimate sacrifice for you.

> **Dear Lord Jesus, I know that I am a sinner, and I ask for Your forgiveness. I believe You died for my sins and rose from the dead. I turn from my sins and invite You to come into my heart and life. I want to trust and follow You as my Lord and Savior.** (The Sinner's Prayer)

Confess with your mouth and believe in your heart the very prayer you just prayed, and you are saved forever from condemnation.

"For the grace of God has been revealed, bringing salvation to all people. And we are instructed to turn from godless living and sinful pleasures. We should live in this evil world with wisdom, righteousness, and devotion to God, while we look forward with hope to that wonderful day when the glory of our great God and Savior, Jesus Christ, will be revealed." (Titus 2:11–13)

Scriptures to study: Isaiah 59:17; Ephesians 6:17; Revelation 7:10.

Journal

Sword of the Spirit

"For the word of God is alive and powerful. It is sharper than the sharpest two-edged sword, cutting between soul and spirit, between joint and marrow. It exposes our innermost thoughts and desires."

Hebrews 4:12

The Word of God is capable of piercing one's heart and attitude. It is also a tool of discernment in the hands of the skilled user.

God refers to the sword of the Spirit as His very breath, His Word, which is living and active right now here on earth. It's the message of hope and of the gospel, God's good news for his people. The sword—the Bible—is a special revelation from God. It is everything that we will ever need. It is His love letter intimately written for you and me.

The Holy Spirit uses the power of God's Word to save souls and then gives us spiritual strength to be mature soldiers for the Lord in fighting the evil in the world we live in. The more we know and understand the Word of God, the more effective we will be in standing against the evil rulers and authorities of the unseen world.

Deuteronomy 8:3 and Matthew 4:4 both tell us that *"People do not live by bread alone, but by every word that comes from the mouth of God."* It is important to memorize scripture and hide it in your heart for when the battle comes, you will know how to fight the good fight.

Scriptures to study: John 1:1–5; 2 Timothy 3:16; Psalm 33:4.

Journal

Believers need to be wary of the devil and protect themselves from his power. However, you do not need to live in fear. The power of the devil is no match for the power of God. The Christian life is not centered on spiritual warfare but on a joyful life of obedience in the Spirit.

Remember our fight is not against flesh-and-blood enemies but against evil rulers and authorities of the unseen world. God's war—God's battle—we have already won! Victory is His!

"Therefore, put on every piece of God's armor so you will be able to resist the enemy in the time of evil.

Then after the battle you will still be standing firm."

(Ephesians 6:13)

Our prayer is that all of you will not give up but will continue your journey of seeking our Lord and Savior and growing in your personal relationship with Jesus.

WAVE
YOUR BANNER
OF FAITH
AND
COMMITMENT
TO THE
LORD

Praise the Lord

(Hallelujah)

Praising the Lord gives God the recognition He deserves. It is an act that we do for Him, keeping our eyes focused on who God is.

"I will exalt you, my God and King, and praise your name forever and ever. I will praise you every day; yes, I will praise you forever. Great is the Lord! He is most worthy of praise! No one can measure his greatness. Let each generation tell its children of your mighty acts; let them proclaim your power. I will meditate on your majestic, glorious splendor and your wonderful miracles. Your awe-inspiring deeds will be on every tongue; I will proclaim your greatness. Everyone will share the story of your wonderful goodness; they will sing with joy about your righteousness. The Lord is merciful and compassionate, slow to get angry and filled with unfailing love. The Lord is good to everyone. He showers compassion on all his creation. All of your works will thank you, Lord, and your faithful followers will praise you. They will speak of the glory of your kingdom; they will give examples of your power. They will tell about your mighty deeds and about the majesty and glory of your reign. For your kingdom is an everlasting kingdom. You rule throughout all generations. The Lord always *keeps his promises; he is gracious in all he does. The Lord helps the fallen and lifts those bent beneath their loads. The eyes of all look to you in hope; you give them their food as they need it. When you open your hand, you satisfy the hunger and thirst of every living thing. The Lord is righteous in everything he does; he is filled with kindness. The Lord is close to all who call on him, yes, to all who call on him in truth. He grants the desires of those who fear him; he hears their cries for help and rescues them. The Lord protects all those who love him, but he destroys the wicked. I will praise the Lord, and may everyone on earth bless his holy name forever and ever.*" (Psalm 145)

Praise Him with thankfulness!

Praise Him with worship!

Praise Him with singing!

Praise Him with lifted hands!

Praise Him with dancing!

Praise Him with instruments!

Praise Him with your words!

Praise Him in fellowship with other believers!

Praise Him in Spirit and in truth for God is Spirit and truth!

Praise Him!

Let the sound of your life resonate that you worship God and have dedicated your life to Him.

This week dig deep into Psalm 145, verse by verse, praying through each one, and pressing into what it means to have God first in your life.

Journal

Sweet Surrender

I surrender Lord! I can't do it anymore! What am I going to do? I need you!

Have you ever gotten to a place in your life where you were defeated, hopeless, and broken? Whether you were the person going to church every Sunday, leading Bible studies, teaching Sunday school, and leading youth group thinking you had it all together, or you were the person living very worldly, plagued with addictions, sexual immorality, doing whatever it took to get ahead, and only thinking of yourself? Perhaps you were the person who lived your life completely apathetic to having any meaning or purpose. You wake up, stick to your routine, don't bother anyone, you're OK with anything, and compromise everything. No matter what your story is or where you find yourself in life, God wants your heart!

A point of surrender is very genuine. It's a time of realness, sadness, vulnerability, desperation, breathlessness, loneliness, fear, anger, helplessness, and so on. It's a place where you finally say, "I give up! I can't do this anymore!" It's a place where your flesh will do whatever it takes to avoid but the very place where God meets you.

"I have called you back from the ends of the earth, saying, "You are my servant." For I have chosen you and will not throw you away. Don't be afraid, for I am with you. Don't be discouraged, for I am your God. I will strengthen you and help you. I will hold you up with my victorious right hand." (Isaiah 41:9–10)

He speaks these words to the depths of your soul in this moment of surrender. Draw near to God, for He IS with you. Repent of your sins and receive the fullness of His mercy, grace, and forgiveness.

God wants to be first in your life. He wants your whole heart. He loves you so much that He rescues you from this desperate place, that point in your life where you cry out to your Father in heaven, and He hears you. He not only hears you, He calls you by name out of the darkness!

He created you in His very own image so He could be everything to you. God knows the world will bring you nothing but darkness, hardship, and despair, but God wants to give you His abundance. As you surrender your life and allow God to sanctify you, you give God access to raise you up, and you become more like Jesus.

Your mind is renewed, your desires and actions change, and your life reflects the fruit of His Spirit. You must actively turn from your old life to live in a new way that pleases God; it is God's grace working in your heart that gives you the desire and power to do so.

Father God, please forgive me. You know how my heart can get so divided and stretched and pulled in ways that are not of you. Thank you for reminding me that You want every single piece of my heart. Please reveal anything I have been turning to instead of You. Teach me to rely on Your strength and power in the areas where I am weak. My deepest desire is to follow steadfast after You.

In Jesus's name, Amen.

Scriptures to study: Psalm 18:6; Matthew 16:24-26; Galatians 2:20.

Journal

Obedience

Is it even possible to live a fully obedient life? Sure it is!

But we are not talking about following a bunch of rules and regulations. The obedience we are talking about is the kind of obedience that is motivated by a changed heart—a heart that loves God more than our own sinful desires, a heart that says no to sin and to my ways and yes to God's ways. God initiates relationships with us and wants us to listen to Him and respond with acts of love in faith. His Word is authoritative and intentional, and it gives profound hope.

> *"And have you forgotten the encouraging words God spoke to you as his children? He said, "My child, don't make light of the Lord's discipline, and don't give up when he corrects you. For the Lord disciplines those he loves, and he punishes each one he accepts as his child."* (Hebrews 12:5-6)

Our earthly fathers' discipline happens only for a few years, doing the best they know how with their limited perspectives until we leave home. God's discipline lasts throughout our lives and is always good for us based on His limitless knowledge and love. Although it is painful, discipline brings a peaceful harvest of right living. Obedience is measured by allowing the Lord's discipline to be effective in your life.

> *"Don't be misled-you cannot mock the justice of God. You will always harvest what you plant. Those who live only to satisfy their own sinful nature will harvest decay*

and death from that sinful nature. But those who live to please the Spirit will harvest everlasting life from the Spirit. So let's not get tired of doing what is good. At just the right time we will reap a harvest of blessing if we don't give up." (Galatians 6:7–9)

An obedient person is submissive to authority and willing to obey. He or she has a healthy fear of the Lord. Those who are obedient know the value of their lives as they understand God's provision, arrangement, and preparation beforehand for the doing of something, the meeting of needs, the supplying of means for the blessing of others. And they always give God the glory!

It is vital that God's believers are extremely obedient and sensitive to the Holy Spirit. As we tell of the good news, which is the hope of Jesus, we are set apart to be that example of God's light in this world. Our motivation for obedience is love!

"If you love me, obey my commandments." (John 14:15)

This week you will notice that you're going to be challenged in obedience. Make the choice to obey every day in the little things.

Scriptures to study: James 1:22–25; Ezekiel 36:26–27; 1 Peter 1:13–16.

Journal

Prayer

Jesus made a way for us to commune with our heavenly Father so that we will have access to the One who created us. God desires our prayers and wants to spend time with us. As we come to Him with open hearts, God creates a place of refuge and safety. As we initiate prayer, God's presence becomes known, and our relationship with God grows the more we experience Him. There is no format, no posture, or form of expression that God requires of us to come to Him in prayer. He simply wants us to come as we are. The innocence of a believer is an act of belief, faith, and trust in the One we come to.

As you experience and encounter God in your prayer time, know that He is always with you and always hears you. Through prayer, God opens eyes, changes hearts, heals wounds, and grants wisdom. Prayer is the key that unlocks the doors to our hearts. Pray for yourself. Pray for your family. Pray for your city or town. Pray for this country. Pray for each other. And in everything, *"always be joyful. Never stop praying. Be thankful in all circumstances, for this is God's will for you who belong to Christ Jesus."* (1 Thessalonians 5:16-18)

God's will for all His people in every circumstance is to rejoice, to pray and to give thanks.

Sometimes there are no words to express what we are going through. *"And the Holy Spirit helps us in our weakness. For example, we don't know what God wants us to pray for. But the Holy Spirit prays for us with groanings that cannot be expressed in words. And the Father who knows all hearts knows what the Spirit is saying, for the Spirit pleads for us believers in harmony with God's own will."* (Romans 8:26–27)

Even Jesus intercedes and pleads for us to our Father in Heaven.

When an army of believers gets together physically or uniting in the Spirit to pray in the mighty name of Jesus, things change, mountains move, waters part, a way is made where it seems impossible. There is power in prayer. We are called to pray for each other, and it pleases God when we do.

As you have read, God wants our prayers. He wants an invitation into our lives, and He wants our praises. God wants full access into our hearts. May our prayers be lifted high in adoration to our Lord and Savior!

Scriptures to study: Matthew 6:9–13; Philippians 4:6–7; Romans 12:12.

Journal

BOW

IN

HUMBLE

ADORATION

Be Humble

God loves a humble heart, a heart that is meek, gentle, compassionate, and kind. A heart that chooses peace over being right, a heart that edifies and builds up, and a heart that loves. When we come to Jesus as sinners, we come in humility. We recognize our lack of worthiness and our complete inability to save ourselves. We acknowledge that we have nothing to offer Him but our sins and our needs for salvation. Jesus humbly gave it all on Calvary, all while displaying the grace and mercy of God. It's that moment when we come to the altar in humble gratitude and lay down our lives to the One who created them, Abba Father!

As believers, we are to live for Christ:

> "You must have the same attitude that Christ Jesus had. Though he was God, he did not think of equality with God as something to cling to. Instead, he gave up his divine privileges; he took the humble position of a slave and was born as a human being. When he appeared in human form, he humbled himself in obedience to God and died a criminal's death on a cross. Therefore, God elevated him to the place of highest honor and gave him the name above all other names." (Philippians 2:5–9)

Jesus took his title and emptied Himself of it as the ultimate expression of divine self-denial. He did not want to cling to his position but gave up His privileges by taking the humble position of a slave. You and I are to follow the same example, giving up all our privileges for the sake of another. To be slaves, the lowly, and the least, and in all of it, stay humble and obedient to God.

God knew that it would be impossible for us to be truly humble without the help of His Holy Spirit. We cannot do it on our own. The more we try, the more we will fail until we daily deny and give up our own special rights, pick up our crosses, yield, and give way to God's voice through the work of the Holy Spirit in our lives. By coming in human form, Jesus knew how much we needed a Savior and what His sole purpose was—to save us from our sins by dying a criminal's death on a cross so that you and I will one day live eternally with our heavenly Father. Jesus humbled Himself, and God lifted Him up in highest honor!

He demonstrated over and over what a humble life looks like. We need to ask God to give us humble hearts and seek to live our lives by Jesus's example so that God will lift us up in honor.

Being humble is having a quiet confidence as we walk through life knowing who we are in Christ Jesus.

Scriptures to study: James 4:10; Philippians 2:3–4; Psalm 149:4.

Journal

Forgiveness

A beautiful word that requires so much yet gives instant mercy. "I'm sorry," to say it and to really mean it. To show empathy, humility, to be genuine, and to show love for another for what you have done or what's been done to you. The action or process of forgiving or to be forgiven. Take the steps in moving in the direction of doing what is good for the sake of freedom in your life. Ask yourself, "Is there any unforgiveness in my heart, or is there someone I need to forgive?"

We need God's help, especially when it comes to forgiveness. We cannot do this without the Holy Spirit and the very cross that made forgiveness possible. Jesus died on the cross to take the sins of the world upon Himself. He chose to look beyond his own pain at the hands of you and me and say, *Father, forgive them, for they don't know what they are doing.*" (Luke 23:34)

Jesus made the ultimate sacrifice, paving the way for us to enter the kingdom to live eternal lives with our heavenly Father.

God knows the stronghold of unforgiveness and what it leads to in your life—anger, resentment, vengeance, bitterness, brokenness, self-righteousness, and pain. When we talk about unforgiveness, we are talking to all of us who justify our own pain. The pain that wasn't our fault, the pain that you suffered at the hands of others, the pain that said you were wrong, the pain that destroyed your family, and the pain that left you abandoned. The pain, the pain, the pain. God knows you have wounds so deep that even the scars are visible, the scars that hurt you, and the scars that consume you. God often allows life to just happen to experience His healing. Jesus's scars were evidence of the crucifixion that He endured on our behalf, and your scars are evidence that you have been healed through Jesus. He wants you to share your story—scars and all—for His glory.

When we forgive, we are deciding to live with the painful consequences of sin and then do it without the bitterness and hatred that threatens to destroy our souls. Don't allow this proud spirit to take root in your life. Don't keep living in your past hurt. To forgive someone is not forgetting or saying, "You're wrong," or saying, "You're right." It's freeing you of bondage from the enemy that has taken hold and kept you bound for too long. Asking for forgiveness, forgiving someone, or forgiving yourself will break the chains that have kept you shackled. If we choose not to forgive or not to receive God's forgiveness, we will continue to live with shame and condemnation, the very things Jesus set us free from. God forgives all who come to Him with a repentant heart. As we humble ourselves, ask for and receive forgiveness, God removes our sins as far from us as the East is from the West.

Take a moment to breathe in God's grace, mercy, forgiveness, and unfailing love. As we come into His presence, pray and take time to evaluate your own heart. *"O Lord, you are so good, so ready to forgive, so full of unfailing love for all who ask for your help."* (Psalm 86:5)

We need to exercise forgiveness every single day. Again, we say the key to forgiveness is the cross. Forgive and be forgiven! Let peace and freedom reign in your heart starting today!

Mathew 18:21-22 says,

> *"Then Peter came to him and asked, "Lord, how often should I forgive someone who sins against me? Seven times?"*
>
> *"No, not seven times," Jesus replied, "but seventy times seven!""*

How many times do we forgive?

All the time with every offense.

Scriptures to study: Acts 13:38; Luke 24:47; Psalm 103.

Journal

Love One Another

It is impossible to truly love one another until you know what love is and that you are loved. *"We know how much God loves us, and we have put our trust in his love. God is love, and all who live in love live in God, and God lives in them."* (1 John 4:16) God is love, and love is God.

Agape love comes directly from our Father. It is God's highest form of love, the love from God for humankind. God created you so you would receive the love He has in its highest form. You cannot love one another if you don't love God and receive His love for you. You cannot give what you don't have. God commands this:

> *"'You must love the Lord your God with all your heart, all your soul, and all your mind.'" This is the first and greatest commandment. A second is equally important: 'Love your neighbor as yourself.' The entire law and all the demands of the prophets are based on these two commandments."* (Matthew 22:37–40)

Jesus came and said all you have to do is to love God with all your existence and love others.

You must understand that we cannot love apart from God. It is when you remain in Jesus (John 15) and the Holy Spirit remains in you that you can bear the fruit of love. The difficult part of loving others is that we often try to do it on our own, whipping up feelings of love where none exist. This can lead to hypocrisy and "play acting" the part of the loving person when our hearts are really cold. Romans 12:9–10 says, *"Don't just pretend to love others. Really love them. Hate what is wrong. Hold tightly to what is good. Love each other with genuine affection, and take delight in honoring each other."* The only way to love one another is by staying fully embraced in God's love and obeying His commands.

Jesus taught us it is by our actions that we show God's love and through our love for others that we are the very image of God. John 13:34–35 says, *"So now I am giving you a new commandment: Love each other. Just as I have loved you, you should love each other. Your love for one another will prove to the world that you are my disciples."* Notice Jesus didn't tell us to feel loving toward one another. He said, "Love each other." He commanded an action, not a feeling. Followers of Jesus are identified by their love for each other.

God calls us to love those that are easy to love as well as the ones that are not so easy to love. Love requires self-sacrifice. You do this by truly becoming concerned about the needs of others and unselfishly giving everything, just as Jesus did. Love is always thinking of others before oneself. Love always extends grace and forgiveness. Love understands and cares about one's eternal life. God loves us all and calls each of us to be a part of His kingdom. We are brothers and sisters in God's eyes. We are family!

Jesus was the very example of God's love. He came to be the Savior of the world. Jesus loved others. He sacrificed His time, efforts, prayer, possessions, and ultimately Himself. God loves us so much that He sacrificed His only Son for you and me. Now that is agape love!

This week we would like you to spend quality time understanding three things:

> God is love.
> God loves you.
> Receive God's love.

Scriptures to study: 1 Corinthians 13:1–7; John 15:9; 1 Peter 4:8.

Journal

BE

THE SALT

AND

LIGHT

IN THIS

WORLD

Sacrifice Is Worship

"This is real love—not that we loved God, but that he loved us and sent his Son as a sacrifice to take away our sins."

1 John 4:10

When we make sacrifices in order to love someone, we get a glimpse of the depth of God's love for us. Love is an action we do for another. So sacrifice for someone else keeps our focus on Jesus, and not ourselves. As we reflect Him in this world, we sacrifice our own desires and interests for the sake and well-being of others. Jesus was always about His Father's business, knowing that His sole purpose was to sacrifice His life, shedding his blood to save us from our sins. God loved us first and wanted us in heaven with Him, a place where there is no more suffering or pain, a place that required the ultimate sacrifice.

Spending time with our Father in prayer enriches our relationship and walk with Him. The more time we spend with Him, the more we become like Jesus. God always orchestrates divine events in our lives for His purpose and His glory. Sometimes our sacrifices are small; sometimes they are big. Either way, the focus is not on us but on who God has placed on our hearts. This is where we need to trust in the leading of the Holy Spirit. You never know how your sacrifice will encourage someone else's walk with Jesus. As believers, our hearts are to see everyone come to know and grow in Jesus as their Lord and Savior. So the sacrifices we can do for our Father are minimal compared to the sacrifice that Jesus gave for you and me.

Psalm 50:14 tells us, *"Make thankfulness your sacrifice to God, and keep the vows you made to the Most High."* We bring the sacrifice of praise before our God. Thankfulness is looking beyond self-interest to express gratitude for His blessings. True sacrifice requires offering one's self to the glory of God, giving ourselves over to Him to do as He pleases. God wants you to make a sacrifice with joy and thankfulness. Let this joy and gladness be the expression of your life. This is where we become a living sacrifice for the Lord. The act of our worship is no longer to bring a sacrifice, but to *be* one, glorifying the Lord in all we do. This is our worship.

We love Jesus for the sacrifice He gave for us, and when we choose to be a light in this dark world, all we can say is shine bright!

> *"Therefore, let us offer through Jesus a continual sacrifice of praise to God, proclaiming our allegiance to his name. And don't forget to do good and to share with those in need. These are the sacrifices that please God."* (Hebrews 13:15–16)

Pray and ask God to highlight those who need your help, and make the sacrifice of what God is telling you to do. Share your worship with your group next week.

Scriptures to study: Romans 12:1-2; Hebrews 10:10; John 4:23-24.

Journal

Serve Others

"And now, Israel, what does the Lord your God require of you?

He requires only that you fear the Lord your God, and live in a way that pleases him, and love him, and serve him with all your heart and soul."

Deuteronomy 10:12

God calls us to serve Him first and then to serve each other. As believers, serving begins with God. He takes precedence over our lives, giving us the ability to serve each other the way that God calls us to. *"For even the Son of Man came not to be served but to serve others and to give his life as a ransom for many."* (Matthew 20:28)

We usually have a hard time serving others before ourselves. We are so focused on our own needs and wants, and even just to have room for others isn't on our radars. We want to be served and have our own needs met. We live in such a me-centered world that, quite frankly, I don't have time to serve you let alone get my day accomplished. For me to meet the needs of someone else, contend with or bear the brunt of someone else's life? My flesh screams, *No way!* How can I bear the load of another when I can hardly bear my own?

How can I meet the needs of someone else when I can't even meet my needs? How can I fathom serving someone else if my life is not in order?

Jesus did not concern Himself with His own needs, wants, or desires. Jesus came to serve others and be the example for our lives. Colossians 3:23–24 says, *"Work willingly at whatever you do, as though you were working for the Lord rather than for people. Remember that the Lord will give you an inheritance as your reward, and that the Master you are serving is Christ."*

Serving others is a sacrifice on our part for the benefit of another.

It is saying:

My love for Jesus overflows from me to you.

I care about you and what you are going through.

I have genuine love for you through Jesus, and my act of compassion for you is the very image of God displayed through me.

God loves me so much that I love you.

You see, God's heart becomes our hearts. His love becomes our love. His compassion becomes our compassion. When we genuinely serve each other, we truly serve the Lord.

As for me and my house, we will serve the Lord!

Scriptures to study: Philippians 2:4; 1 Peter 4:10; Luke 12:35–38.

Journal

Overflowing Joy

God is the source of true joy! It is an expression of God's goodness that is deeply rooted and inspired by the Holy Spirit. This joy is a presence that overwhelms you to a place of complete peace. This kind of joy can only be given by our Father in heaven. *"When you obey my commandments, you remain in my love, just as I obey my Father's commandments and remain in his love. I have told you these things so that you will be filled with my joy. Yes, your joy will overflow!"* (John 15:10–11)

Christian joy is rooted in a person's relationship with the Lord, and it is resilient even in the midst of suffering and death. No matter where you are in life, on the top of the highest mountain or in the lowest of valleys or anywhere in between, The Joy of the Lord is your strength. Joy is not based on our circumstances or our happiness. Joy comes from knowing that whatever happens, God will use everything for our ultimate good. It unlocks a sense of purpose and hope and gives us an overflowing well of joy that shifts our focus on kingdom desires, not worldly circumstances.

How wonderful life can be if we only live by our object of faith, Jesus. Luke 12:31 says, *"Seek the Kingdom of God above all else, and he will give you everything you need."* Love, joy, peace, patience, kindness, goodness, faithfulness, gentleness, and self-control are all gifts produced by the Holy Spirit. As you examine the fruit in your own life, do you look to the one and only Jesus to produce the very gift of joy that God wants to give you? Make Jesus the object that matters, and He will give you all you could ever need. The more we, as disciples, abide in Christ, the more we will bear the fruit of Christ. Do you know that God's joy is grounded in the wonder of His divine love for you? Just as parents find joy in their children because of the deep love they have for them, so much more does God love you. And this love bond is something that can never be broken. You see, the real secret to a joyful life is in being continuously, "filled with the Spirit of God." If you desire more joy in your life, then your heart's desire is to seek out our Lord and Savior Jesus and keep drawing nearer to Him.

Joy comes in the morning!

Wake up fresh every day with a joy that is contagious! A joy that says, "I'm a child of the King!"

Scriptures to study: Matthew 7:7–11; Galatians 5:22–25; 1 Thessalonians 5:16.

Journal

Freedom

Wow! I just want to scream it out loud! "Freedom!" What joy, what peace is given to those who have experienced freedom.

"God decided in advance to adopt us into his own family by bringing us to himself through Jesus Christ. This is what he wanted to do, and it gave him great pleasure. So we praise God for the glorious grace he has poured out on us who belong to his dear Son. He is so rich in kindness and grace that he purchased our freedom with the blood of his Son and forgave our sins." (Ephesians 1:5–7)

We are heirs to eternal life through Jesus. We are signed, sealed, and delivered. Make it personal. I'm His!

As believers we need to pray for an understanding of how to walk out this life on earth in freedom. You can ask yourself right now, "What do I need freed from? What keeps me bound? What keeps me down? What keeps me going around the same mountain?" You don't have to live in bondage because of your situation. You can live your life in freedom because of Jesus, who is in the midst of your situation. God made a way for us. Believe it! Please understand when we say that this life is not easy. We certainly know the struggles that life can bring. You need to *want* freedom in your life. You cannot have one foot in heaven and one foot in the world and expect to have freedom. God promises to restore what was taken, to replace what was stolen, to repair what was broken. Ask our gracious heavenly Father for freedom, and receive healing over those areas in your life. Repent and surrender to our loving Father, who gladly takes your sin and casts it as far as the East is from the West. He takes your brokenness and fully restores and heals you as you humbly walk this journey of life with our Lord and Savior, Jesus. Put on your eternal eyes! Freedom for Christians is always a means to a greater end!

Every day we need a fresh surrender to the Holy Spirit (our helper). *"For the Lord is the Spirit, and wherever the Spirit of the Lord is, there is freedom."* (2 Corinthians 3:17) Let me say that again. Every day we need a fresh surrender to the Holy Spirit.

"For the Lord is the Spirit, and wherever the Spirit of the Lord is, there is freedom." Have faith in the Spirit's sufficiency to surrender, and trust His empowerment. Jesus lives in you to empower you with an unleashing of divine joy. Believe Him! Have faith in Him! Trust Him! Experience God! Experience freedom!

Scriptures to study; Galatians 5:13; John 8:31-32; Psalm 119:45.

Journal

Rest in Him

"Then Jesus said, "Come to me, all of you who are weary and carry heavy burdens, and I will give you rest. Take my yoke upon you. Let me teach you, because I am humble and gentle at heart, and you will find rest for your souls. For my yoke is easy to bear, and the burden I give you is light."

Matthew 11:28–30

Come and let: This is an invitation. Jesus invites us into a refreshing spiritual rest.

Give: Jesus supplies this very rest.

Humble: This is the very essence of who Jesus is.

Gentle: It's His loving tenderness.

Easy and light: It's uncomplicated.

Jesus provides this special rest for you and me. There is freedom in this rest. Not because life is less demanding but because the power of Jesus, by the Holy Spirit, makes it possible for us to enter into His rest. We become one with the Lord through His Spirit and enter into His presence. In that moment is where we will find spiritual rest. Take His yoke upon you, and rest in Him daily.

Here is where we gain refreshing spiritual rest, knowing that He is completely sovereign over our lives.

Here you will receive all that Jesus has for you.

Here is where we walk in humility.

Here is where love grows.

Here is where you let go and let God.

This special rest is a place where you meet with God, and He meets with you. And you are forever changed. For only we who believe can enter his rest.

Scriptures to study: Isaiah 11:2; Jeremiah 6:16: Hebrews 4

Journal

Printed in the United States
by Baker & Taylor Publisher Services